Table of Conten

The Need for this Book ....

About the author 3

Mild Graphic Content Warning..4

Racial Disparities..5

Finality and Irreversibility 7

Income Inequality 8

Mixed Signals 10

Inadequate Legal Representation..11

Inhumanity..14

The Catholic Pope 18

Vengefulness..19

Public Opinion..20

Deterrent Effect 22

Executing the Innocent 27

Life in Prison is worse than Death Penalty 29

Arbitrary Application 30

Excluding Abolitionist Jurors..31

Other Countries 32

Saving Money..33

Life Sentence as Suitable Alternative 34

Conclusion..36

The Need for this Book

The university where I teach has roughly 50 books on the death penalty. About half are anti-death penalty and the other half are neutral. There is not a single book that principally argues for capital punishment. As the title suggests, this book is designed to fill that gap.

This book is structured to provide detailed analysis in a concise, easy-to-follow format. I am confident that, no matter the reader's frame of reference, this book will illuminate this controversial topic. Even anti-death penalty advocates will benefit greatly by being exposed to the criticisms of their position (and thus become better equipped to address those criticisms and avoid common pitfalls).

Please note that every footnote provided gives further details on the specific topic it is associated with. They are not just references to sources. The reader can simply read the main text for a faster experience, but I encourage you to also read the footnotes on topics that interest you.

I will gladly respond to any constructive feedback left in an Amazon review.

About the author

Michael Conklin has been teaching Business Law at the university level for over 10 years. He participates in many special-event lectures and debates over legal, political, and philosophical issues, including the death penalty. Living in Colorado, he enjoys mountaineering and photography.

Mild Graphic Content Warning

Abolitionists conveniently fail to mention details about the murders committed by the people they claim don't deserve capital punishment. But how can people be expected to make an informed decision on a punishment's validity without knowing what the person is being punished for? You must have both sides of the equation to make an informed decision. Therefore, this book occasionally mentions the crimes committed by those receiving capital punishment. The reader is spared the most gruesome of details, but a moderate level of specificity is provided.

Racial Disparities

Abolitionists are quick to point out that, compared to the overall population, a disproportionate number of African Americans are executed. While true, this is a very deceptive use of a statistic.

The problem with using this statistic as evidence of a racist legal system is illustrated by a far more disproportionate statistic: Men make up only 49 percent of the U.S. population, but 98.5 percent of those executed are males. Does this prove that our legal system is exceedingly sexist against men? Obviously not; it's simply a function of the differences between male and female behaviors.

There are other, more revealing race-related statistics that abolitionists conveniently never mention. According to a Department of Justice study, African Americans make up 48 percent of those charged with homicide, but only 41 percent of those who were sentenced to death. Another inconvenient statistic for those trying to prove racism is that a white person on death row is more likely to be executed than an African American. Furthermore, white people on death row are executed faster than African Americans. In other words, African Americans on trial for murder are less likely to be given the death penalty, and less likely to be executed when given the death penalty. It would be a very peculiar argument to claim a legal system with these results is racist against African Americans.

The abolitionist's logic on the issue is clear: If a punishment has a racial disparity, then we should not allow that punishment. When this logic is applied consistently, the results are clearly untenable. If the desired result of eliminating the death penalty were achieved, it wouldn't stop there. Life sentences are also a punishment with a racial disparity. Therefore, the abolitionist's logic would also require eliminating that punishment – same with 40-year sentences, 30-year sentences, 20-year sentences, etc.[1]

---

[1] This is a textbook example of the taxi cab fallacy. This occurs when someone evokes a principle to reach a desired outcome and then inconsistently abandons

The Supreme Court addressed the issue of racial disparities in the 1987 case of *McCleskey v. Kemp*. Warren McCleskey was a career criminal who killed a police officer by shooting him in the head during an armed robbery. McCleskey's legal team appealed to the Supreme Court trying to save their client from the death penalty, but not because he didn't do it. Rather, because racial disparities exist in death penalty cases. The Court held that race-based sentencing disparities are "an inevitable part of our criminal justice system." Furthermore, the Court pointed out that what McCleskey was requesting would require a "totally unrealistic condition" to capital cases. The study used by McCleskey's legal team as evidence of racism, the Baldus study, was held to "not demonstrate a constitutionally significant risk of racial bias" by the Supreme Court.

Another crime statistic that is rarely discussed is that minorities are significantly more likely to be the victim of a capital offense. Therefore, the deterrent effect of the death penalty disproportionately benefits this group.

A simple question can be posed to the abolitionist to uncover their real motive behind using the race argument, "If the death penalty was perfectly proportional, would you still oppose it?" The answer will always be "Yes." So this racial aspect they bring up is irrelevant to their desire regarding the elimination of the death penalty.

---

that principle afterwards. Principles are not taxi cabs that can be dismissed when one reaches a desired result.

Finality and Irreversibility

Abolitionists will often point out that the death penalty should be abolished because it is irreversible. But when asked for an example of an execution that should be reversed because the executed was innocent, they are hard-pressed to present one (see "Executing the Innocent" chapter).

The finality of the death penalty is a strength, not a weakness. As discussed in the "Life Sentence as Suitable Alternative" chapter, life in prison without the possibility of parole does not guarantee that a murderer will not kill again. Likewise, the death penalty is the only way for the victim's family and community to get the closure they deserve.

Furthermore, many punishments have an element of irreversibility to them. If someone dies in prison and they are later found to have been wrongly convicted, nothing can be done to change that. Even if the truth is discovered during the lifetime of the person wrongfully convicted, nothing can undo what has been done. For example, if someone is discovered to have been wrongly convicted after serving his 20s and 30s in prison, you can release him and give monetary compensation, but you can never give him back his 20s and 30s. Consequently, if the abolitionist wants to eliminate punishments because they are not reversible, this logic would apply to much more than just the death penalty.

Income Inequality

It is true that, relative to the general population, people below the poverty line are executed at a higher rate. The following quote from abolitionist Jeffrey Reiman is a common sentiment on the issue:

> If poverty in America is unjust, and if murder is a predictable result of this unjust poverty, then the society that refuses to remedy this poverty bears some responsibility for the murders that result... the vast majority of murders in America are a predictable response to the frustrations and disabilities of impoverished social circumstances, and that that impoverishment is a remediable injustice from which others in America benefit, American society bears some of the responsibility for these murders and thus has no right to exact the full cost of murders from its murderers...

This quote admits that poor people commit murders at a disproportionally higher rate than other socioeconomic groups, thus their higher incarceration rate. But it then makes the jump that the poor people who commit these murders are not fully responsible for their actions. Common sense dictates that a strategy of reducing the responsibility of the group that commits the most murders will lead to more murders.

More importantly, the author presents no evidence to support his claim that poverty and income inequality somehow stand in causal relation to crime. To the contrary, there was no appreciable rise in crime from the roaring 1920's to The Great Depression where unemployment was 25%. Likewise, during The Great Recession from 2008-2010, where the unemployment rate doubled, crime actually went down, reaching a 40-year low in 2010. Furthermore, there is no correlation between income inequality and crime. Income inequality significantly increased from 1980 to present. However, the crime rate has correspondingly decreased in this same time period.

Some imaginative defense attorneys have tried to use their client's lack of wealth to evade responsibility for their actions. In one such example, a defendant who raped and sexually tortured multiple victims was described as Jean Valjean, the honest peasant from "Les Miserables." The defense attorney went on to claim that, like Valjean, his client only committed crimes "to feed his family." The details of how sexually torturing people helps one feed his family were absent. I am not aware of any capital case in the last 40 years where the defendant was only trying to feed his family. And even if a case like this did exist, that motivation would be taken into consideration as a mitigating factor during the sentencing stage of the trial, and would certainly exclude any possibility of the death penalty.

As illustrated previously in the Racial Disparities chapter, if that standard for eliminating the death penalty was consistently applied to other punishments, they would need to be abolished as well. This income inequality argument suffers the same fate.

To illustrate this, look at the abolitionist quote presented at the beginning of this chapter. It would equally apply to other crimes such as assault: "If poverty in America is unjust, and if [assault] is a predictable result of this unjust poverty, then the society that refuses to remedy this poverty bears some responsibility for the [assaults] that result..." Therefore, if this abolitionist is consistent, his argument would not only apply to murderers, but also robbers, rapists, and vandals.

Mixed Signals

This is the most peculiar abolitionist argument I have been confronted with. The most coherent summation is that the government tells people not to kill, but then sometimes the government kills. Supposedly, this sends mixed signals to criminals and they become confused as to whether they should murder or not. The problem, of course, is trying to equate the brutal killing of an innocent person with the painless death of a murderer (to protect against them killing again).

This argument is further diminished by the fact that the death penalty represents a very small portion of killing done by the government. The police kill roughly 1,000 people a year, compared to 20-30 killed by executions. Should we also take away police officers' guns in an effort to clear up any confusion as to whether citizens are allowed to murder?

Arguing against the death penalty because it confuses criminals is the intellectual equivalent of arguing against incarcerating kidnappers because that's like the government kidnapping them.

Inadequate Legal Representation

The abolitionist is quick to recount anecdotes of defense attorneys falling asleep at trial. I can only speculate that nodding off is the accusation of choice because it is impossible to disprove (as opposed to something in the trial record). Often it's an anti-death penalty journalist (who would be sitting behind the attorney) who makes the claim.

Ineffective assistance of counsel has been referred to as "the most common arrow in the quiver of a desperate convict."[2] The truth is that, in every capital case, the plaintiff and defense attorneys, if given the chance, would do multiple things differently. Trying a case is not an exact science. Some tactics are effective with certain juries, judges, and defendants, but not with others. It's easy to "Monday morning quarterback" and criticize an attorney after watching a biased 10-minute news segment.[3]

---

[2] A story from my former law professor illustrates the frequency of desperate defendants claiming ineffective assistance of counsel. During his first month as a criminal defense attorney, one of his clients stood up in court and went on a tirade about his attorney's supposed incompetence. He was so embarrassed that afterward he went over to the prosecutor to rehabilitate his reputation. The prosecutor just laughed and said, "Don't worry about it. This is the second time that's happened today!"

[3] Another example of abolitionists' desperate use of an ineffective assistance of counsel claim is illustrated by the Death Penalty Information Center in their May 30, 2017 podcast. They describe eight convicted murderers in Arkansas who were scheduled to be executed in a 10-day period. They claimed ineffective assistance of counsel because the prison was an hour away from where the attorneys were, and this made it difficult for them to meet their clients as frequently as they would like in the days leading up to the execution.

Note that this ineffective assistance of counsel claim came just days before the scheduled execution. With only one exception, this was over 20 years after the convictions and after all trial-related appeals had long-sense been exhausted. The only one who was convicted less than 20 years ago, Kenneth Williams, is a cautionary tale about the difference between a life sentence and the death penalty. After killing a University of Arkansas cheerleader, he was spared the death penalty and was instead sentenced to life. He later escaped and killed two more victims while out. This time he was sentenced to death and executed in 2017, ensuring that he will never kill again.

Defendants in capital cases receive, at minimum, the same legal representation afforded to non-capital murder trials, and often it is far superior. Timothy McVeigh received a $6 million legal defense. He then filed an appeal based on ineffective assistance of counsel, even though he always maintained he did the bombing. It's important to note that death penalty abolitionists want McVeigh (who was executed in 2001) to be alive and well. His $6 million legal defense, the 168 people he murdered, and the devastation he caused to the Oklahoma City community are literally irrelevant to the abolitionist's desire to end the death penalty. So again, the reason provided by the abolitionist (inadequate legal representation) is superfluous.

The problem with claiming ineffective assistance of council is that you must show "a reasonable probability that, but for counsel's unprofessional errors, the result of the proceeding would have been different." The Supreme Court case that led to this standard, *Strickland v. Washington*, is illustrative. David Leroy Washington killed three people on three different days. He stabbed a sleeping 69-year-old minister seven times, shot and stabbed a woman in order to steal $8, and then tied a 20-year-old college student to a bed and stabbed him 11 times while he begged for his life. Washington confessed to the murders and admitted he had no excuse. "I had all the best breaks in life, all the right opportunities." He pleaded guilty at trial and during the sentencing phase, his defense attorney decided not to provide the mitigating circumstance that the murders were caused by Washington's stressful home life. This strategic decision was made in part because bringing this up would open Washington to cross-examination and would expose his prior criminal record. After sentenced to death, Washington tried to appeal based on ineffective assistance of counsel. In an 8-1 decision, the Supreme Court rejected his claim.[4]

Even if it is granted that occasionally a capital defendant receives an inadequate legal defense, it's a tenuous connection to posit that therefore every murderer on death row should not receive their

[4] The only dissenting justice, Marshall, didn't dissent because he thought Washington received ineffective assistance of counsel. Rather, because he disagreed with the practicality of the standards set by the majority.

punishment. If a few people who were sentenced to life in prison were found to have received ineffective assistance of counsel, should we commute the sentence of every lifer? A far more common-sense approach is what we currently do: Allow convicted murderers to appeal based on ineffective assistance of counsel (free of charge). And if the courts find that their legal representation had some "reasonable probability" of changing the outcome of the case, then they are provided a new trial with new legal representation.[5]

Whenever I am confronted with an abolitionist making allegations of sleeping attorneys, I simply ask what that attorney would have done, had he been awake, to change the outcome of the trial. This question has never been met with a single example.[6]

---

[5] Remember, the standard is not a "reasonable possibility" that a better attorney would have proved their innocence. The criminal justice system is not built on proving innocence. The standard is far less than that. They only need to show that a better attorney might have created some reasonable doubt in one of the twelve jurors. This is an incredibly defendant-friendly standard.

[6] I do want to clarify that there have certainly been people convicted of a capital crime in the U.S. who received ineffective assistance of counsel (and were not given a new trial). The abolitionist is quick to bring these up. However, these legitimate examples are often from the early 1900s. Our discussion as to whether we should have the death penalty *today* should be limited to outcomes in, at least, the last 30 years. If we abolish punishments today based on injustices involving those punishments 100 years ago, we would have to abolish everything.

Inhumanity

In considering the potential inhumanity of lethal injection, it is important to compare it to the crime that was committed (something abolitionists conveniently leave out of the equation). Yes, it would be inhumane to execute a person who stole $20 or cheated on his taxes. But when you contrast lethal injection (which is preceded by a last meal, the opportunity to have a discussion with a religious leader, the ability to say goodbye to loved ones, etc.) to the way that person killed his victims, the comparative humanity becomes clear.[7] When you understand the evil actions that death-row inmates have done (and their often utterly unrepentant attitude toward them), it becomes clear that the death penalty is an act of mercy, sparing the murderer from a more proportionate punishment.

In the Supreme Court case of *Glossip v. Gross*, abolitionists challenged Oklahoma's use of midazolam instead of the standard sodium thiopental in lethal injections. They gave sensationalist accounts of how using midazolam resulted in an extremely painful death. However, after looking at the evidence, the Supreme Court and district court both disagreed. They held that there is a "virtual certainty" that prisoners will feel no pain and rejected the abolitionist's "speculative evidence" that it might cause pain.

There is a dark side behind the case of *Glossip v. Gross* that few are aware of. The reason Oklahoma switched to the controversial midazolam method of execution was the direct result of abolitionist's successful efforts to pressure suppliers of the standard drugs not to supply them.

---

[7] Some abolitionists claim that the relative suddenness of a murderer's victim's death is preferable to the foreseen death the murderer faces. As leading abolitionist Jeffrey Reiman demonstrates, "...execution involves the most psychologically painful features of death.... We normally regard death whose coming is foreseen by its victim as worse than sudden death because a foreseen death adds to the loss of life the terrible consciousness of that impending loss." Abolitionist Albert Camus seconds this notion, "Two deaths are inflicted on [those executed], the first being worse than the second, whereas [the murderer being executed] killed but once."

The petitioner was confronted about this in oral arguments when Justice Scalia asked, "[The previous methods were] rendered unavailable by the abolitionist movement... and now you want to come before the Court and say, 'well this third drug is not 100% sure.' The reason it is not 100% sure is because the abolitionists have rendered it impossible to get the 100% sure drugs." The petitioner representing the murderers on death row said the answer to that was not relevant.

Directly counter to the abolitionist's claim, the existence of the death penalty demonstrates a recognition of human dignity. It shows how much we value the humanity of those who have been negatively affected by the murderer. Simply put, by reducing the punishment for particularly heinous murders, you illustrate that you view the crime (and its effects) as less significant.

Another reason for the abolitionist position that execution methods are inhumane is that they don't acknowledge, or are unaware, that it prevents future murders (as explained in the Deterrence chapter). After all, most abolitionists are fine with self-defense killings.

It is interesting to note that many anti-death penalty advocates are supporters of assisted suicide. There, they are quick to point out that the process is painless. Yet when it comes to the death penalty, these same people attempt to cast doubt on whether it is possible to painlessly execute someone.[8]

A strong case can be made that, even if you refuse to consider the humanity of preventing future murders and providing closure to the families and communities that have been devastated by a murderer, the death penalty is still humane because it treats murderers as autonomous agents. Autonomy is part of our humanity. A life sentence for Timothy McVeigh would be far less than what he deserves and therefore is not

---

[8] This inconsistency can also be pointed out by asking the abolitionist to provide a more humane method of execution. If they can't, this means, by definition, that we use the most humane method available. This will have no effect on the abolitionist's opposition to the death penalty, which proves that the method of execution, despite them bringing it up, is not relevant. They will remain opposed regardless of the method.

holding him responsible for his actions. Consequently, this denies him his autonomy, and therefore also his humanity.

Abolitionists sometimes point out that there are still executions by hanging and firing squad in the United States. Much less frequent is their acknowledgement that every instance of this in the last 50 years was the result of the convict choosing that form of execution.[9]

Somewhat related to the issue of the humanity of executions is the way many abolitionists view the murderers on death row. The more you study the writings of leading abolitionists, the more you come to realize that they don't think the heinous murders mentioned in this book are that bad.[10] Abolitionist Jeffrey Reiman illustrates: "I cannot see how a sentence that would require a murderer to spend... the twenty years between age thirty and age fifty [in prison], can be regarded as anything less than extremely severe and thus no trivialization of the harm he has caused." I doubt Reiman would be consistent if it was his family brutally murdered and tortured. If he saw the person responsible twenty years later enjoying himself with his family, while Reiman's family remain dead, I doubt he would say, "Well, he has already received an *extremely severe* punishment; I don't feel that the harm he caused me is trivialized at all!"

---

[9] There's an interesting history behind these choices. Billy Bailey, a career criminal who murdered an elderly couple in their home for no reason, chose hanging over lethal injection stating, "I'm not going to let them put me to sleep." Utah's use of allowing prisoners to choose the firing squad has roots in their Mormon background. The blood atonement doctrine (which is no longer taught in Mormonism), teaches that some crimes are so bad that the atonement of Jesus is not enough. To atone for these sins, the perpetrator's blood must be shed.

[10] An excellent analogy for how leading abolitionists view murderers, as juxtaposed to their victims, is presented by Louis P. Pojman. He uses a contemporary version of the good Samaritan story to illustrate:

A man is brutally robbed and left on the side of the road by his assailants. A priest comes by but regrets having to leave the man in his condition, in order to avoid being late for the church service he must lead. Likewise, a lawyer passes by, rushing to meet a client. Finally, a psychiatrist sees our subject, rushes over to him, places the man's head in his lap and in a distraught voice cries out, "Oh, this is awful! How deplorable! Tell me, sir, who did this to you? He needs help."

The notion that the murders committed by those on death row are really not that bad, while surprising, is common among abolitionists. I participated in a public debate on the death penalty with an ACLU attorney and received a very telling question from my opponent: "Which is worse, the monstrous crimes that men commit, or the barbarous ways that we punish them?" While happy to be given such an easy question, I was shocked because this was a prepared statement, not an accidental slip of the tongue. This abolitionist, who had researched the issue, genuinely thought that receiving lethal injection after being convicted of a brutal murder and exhausting all available appeals, was worse than the brutal killing of the innocent person that led to the lethal injection.[11]

[11] One explanation for such an extreme position is that the abolitionists want to distance themselves as far as they can from their opposition. Since death penalty advocates (their opposition) talk negatively about convicted murderers on death row, the abolitionist, in a contrarian attempt to differentiate themselves, feel the need to downplay these crimes.

The Catholic Pope

The Catholic Church has executed hundreds of people for hundreds of years. Compared to the modern-day death penalty in the United States, those executed by the Church were guilty of far less severe offenses, had a burden of proof far less favorable to the defendant, received fewer legal protections, were provided fewer abilities to appeal, and were executed by methods fare more cruel.

The current pope, Pope Francis, is against the death penalty "no matter how serious the crime committed." He states that the death penalty "contradicts God's plan for man and society." This is a peculiar position to be espoused by the head of a religion whose holy book explicitly condones the practice. Pope Francis also advocates for abolishing life sentences no matter how atrocious the crime (a position many death penalty abolitionists support, but are reluctant to publicly acknowledge).

Abolitionists pointing out that the pope is against the death penalty is a textbook example of the fallacy of appeal to authority. Whether or not this one person in Europe is for or against the death penalty is irrelevant. This can quickly be illustrated by asking the abolitionist, "If the pope was for the death penalty, would that make it right?"

The only relevance to the pope's stance would be if he provided a convincing argument for his position. His attempts at doing so thus far have only resulted in the assertion that it violates the "life and dignity of the human person," and that "There is no humane way of killing another person." Researching the pope's comments on the death penalty also reveal that he does not acknowledge the reality of its deterrent effect.

Vengefulness

Bryan Stevenson explains this abolitionist position, "The logic of gratuitously killing someone to demonstrate that killing is wrong eludes me. We don't rape those who rape, nor do we assault those who have assaulted. We disavow torturing those who have tortured. Yet we endorse killing those who have killed."

This is a false equivalency on many levels. First, Stevenson assumes part of what he is trying to prove when he asserts that the death penalty is "gratuitous killing." Second, we don't even come close to doing to convicted murderers what they have done to their victims. For example, Angel Diaz stabbed and strangled a man to death with his own shoelaces. Then, after stopping to snack on donuts, raped the man's wife and 16-year-old daughter, sexually torturing them with various items including a curling iron and umbrella, all while a 3-year-old watched from her crib.[12] To claim that executing this type of person by lethal injection is in any way equivalent to what he did to his victims, demonstrates either an intentional deception, or an inability to make the most elementary of distinctions.

The vengeful accusation is often rooted in the assumption that the death penalty is completely "gratuitous." Meaning, life in prison without the possibility of parole is just as effective at deterring future crime. As shown in the "Life Sentence as Suitable Alternative" chapter, this is patently false.

---

[12] This is the murderer referred to previously in this book because his attorney attempted the "Les Miserables Defense." Despite being only 18 at the time, Diaz had already been convicted four times for burglaries, robberies, and assault. Diaz's attorney requested a 3-week adjournment so that his client could marry his girlfriend. The judge refused. The defense attorney then attempted to liken Diaz to Jean Valjean, the honest peasant from "Les Miserables." Mr. Diaz only committed these crimes "to feed his family," claimed the attorney.
He is not to be confused with Angel Nieves Diaz, who was executed for murdering a strip club owner during a robbery. Surprisingly, this latter Angel Diaz received more media attention than the former.

Public Opinion

When it comes to opinion polls, abolitionists often try and distort reality to make their side appear more popular. The truth is, for the last 50 years, significantly more Americans favor than oppose the death penalty. Even this result is based on survey phrasing that is biased in favor of the abolitionist's position, such as, "Are you in favor of the death penalty for a person convicted of murder?" This wording implies that an affirmative answer supports the death penalty for all convicted murderers when in reality we only execute the worst of the worst: about 1 in 1,000 murderers. It would be like asking, "Are you in favor of 20 year prison sentences for larceny?" Most people would say "No." And yet in extreme cases where a career criminal stole an $800,000 diamond by putting the lives of others at risk, many of those same people would want a 20 year term as an option.

Another example of the biased phrasing often used in these surveys to make the results appear to favor the abolitionist is, "If convicted murderers in this state could be sentenced to life in prison with absolutely no chance of ever being released on parole or returning to society, would you prefer this as an alternative to the death penalty?" As demonstrated in the chapter, "Life Sentence as Suitable Alternative," this question is complete fiction. Even I, the author of this pro-capital punishment book, would consider answering in the affirmative.

When these surveys use an unbiased question, the results are even more drastically in favor of the death penalty. An example of a neutrally phrased question is, "Among persons convicted of first degree murder," should the death penalty be given to "all," "no one," or whether it "should depend on the circumstances of the case and the character of the person." When this more realistic question is asked, the percent of Americans who say no one should be executed is frequently less than 20%.

It's puzzling when abolitionists reference public opinion polls because it is their side that desires to take the decision away from the public. When the people of a state decide to abolish the death penalty, pro-capital punishment advocates don't seek to use the courts to circumvent the will of the voters. The abolitionists, however, want to have it both ways. When the people of a state want to do away with the death penalty, they agree. But when the populace wants the death penalty, they work to deny them that choice. Since the abolitionist's position is to end the death penalty regardless of what the people want, it is peculiar that they bring up the issue of public opinion.

It's also interesting to note that the overwhelming public support for the death penalty is despite the constant one-sided portrayal in the media. The media's portrayal is somewhat understandable given the fact that more sensational stories attract more viewers. A story about a brutal murderer being executed and the corresponding deterrent effect and closure it provided the victim's surviving family will not get as many viewers as a story about an "innocent" man about to be executed.

The same "sensationalism sells" plays a part in why movies are overwhelmingly anti-death penalty. But regardless of the explanation, the fact remains that the media's portrayal of the death penalty is overwhelmingly distorted in favor of the abolitionist's position. Popular movies about the death penalty include, "The Life of David Gale" with Kevin Spacey, "True Crime" with Clint Eastwood, "Dead Man Walking" with Sean Penn, "The Green Mile" with Tom Hanks, "12 Angry Men," and Stanley Kubrick's "Paths of Glory." Every one of those are anti-death penalty movies. After extensive searching, I was unable to find a single major motion picture that was pro-capital punishment; even movies with neutral depictions of the death penalty are hard to come by.

Literature on the subject is also skewed. At the university library where I teach, there are roughly 50 books on the death penalty. At least half are anti-death penalty and the other half are neutral (either point-counterpoint books that present both sides, or books that simply document facts and court cases). There is not a single book that principally argues for the necessity of the death penalty.

Deterrent Effect

Because we cannot perform experiments that recreate death penalty scenarios, the statistics on both sides are speculative. However, one thing is absolutely certain: The death penalty, unequivocally, deters future crimes. While convicted murderers who were not executed sometimes kill again, there has never been a single example of an executed murderer killing again. In this way, the death penalty is not only a proven deterrent, it is the *ultimate* deterrent. As explained in the "Life Sentence as Suitable Alternative" chapter, anything short of the death penalty increases the likelihood of additional murders. While this settles the deterrence issue, I will go on to address the distinction between specific and general deterrence.

Specific deterrence would be an executed murderer never being able to murder again. General deterrence would be fewer murders in the general population. Abolitionists like to exclude the undeniable case of specific deterrence and focus on the less clear general deterrence effect.[13] Given the limits of statistical analysis, we will never know with absolute certainty the general deterrence effects.[14] But common sense, human nature, and available statistics all strongly point to a general deterrence effect.

---

[13] It should be pointed out that some abolitionists make a distinction, not between general and specific deterrence, but, rather, between deterrence and incapacitation. This way, the executed murderer can be excluded from the deterrence effect because he was not deterred from killing again; rather, he was incapacitated from doing so. This is a distinction without a relevant difference. When people talk about deterrence, they are talking about whether or not the death penalty will have a favorable effect on future murders (which it clearly does). Put another way, if your loved one was murdered, it would likely make no difference to you if they were murdered by someone who was not deterred or someone who was not incapacitated.

[14] This is a classic example of the difference between the seen and the unseen. Judge Human Barshay explains this way: "The death penalty is a warning, just like a lighthouse throwing its beams out to sea. We hear about shipwrecks, but we do not hear about the ships the lighthouse guides safely on their way."

Many people view criminals as crazed maniacs who commit all their crimes based on an uncontrollable impulse with no regard for risk assessment. In reality, the criminal element is actually fairly rational.[15] For example, when laws are altered to add additional prison terms if a firearm is used during a crime, criminals are less likely to use a gun. When mandatory sentencing laws for various drugs are changed, criminals alter their behavior accordingly. In areas with high gun ownership, criminals are more likely to wait until the homeowner is gone before attempting to break in. Simply put, the more severe a punishment, the less of that behavior you get on average.[16] Remember, to demonstrate a general deterrent effect, there is no burden to show that *every* murder would be deterred, or even that a large number would, just that some will.[17]

Abolitionists will sometimes claim that any general deterrence effect will be negligible because murders are often crimes of passion where there's no time for rational thought (such as walking in on a cheating spouse and killing them). This objection (that the deterrent effect is "negligible") acknowledges that the death penalty deters *some* murders. More importantly, this shows a lack of understanding about who receives the death penalty. Heat-of-passion murders are generally tried as second-degree murder where the death penalty is never an option. And again, the abolitionist wastes his time showing that *some* murders (or even *most*

---

[15] Democratic Senator Dianne Feinstein demonstrates one such example with the following interaction: "...I saw that she carried a weapon that was unloaded into a grocery store robbery. I asked her the question: 'Why was the gun unloaded?' She said to me: 'So I would not panic, kill somebody, and get the death penalty.' That was firsthand testimony directly to me that the death penalty in place in California [at the time] was in fact a deterrent."

[16] One comparison sometimes implemented to illustrate this point is the every-other-day analogy. Pretend that the United States enacted a nationwide policy that banned the death penalty for murders committed on odd-numbered days, while allowing it for murders committed on even-numbered days. This would clearly result in more murders committed on odd-numbered days. Note that for a lot of murderers, maybe even most, this policy would have no effect. The analogy only needs to show that *some* murderers would alter their behavior.

[17] A telling admission on the subject comes straight from the source: Carl Isaacs, who murdered 15 people, said from his death-row cell, "If they want to stop me, they'd better strap me in that chair, because my ambition is to kill 1,000 people.... As long as killers know all they'll get is life, they'll keep right on killing—and that includes me." The Death Penalty in America p. 133

murders) would not be deterred by the death penalty. A general deterrence effect exists if just *some* murders are deterred.

An example of the misapplication of statistics comes courtesy of the Death Penalty Information Center. They state, "Nationwide murder rates undermine the deterrence hypothesis. The South, the region with the most executions, actually has the highest murder rate, while the Northeast, the region with the fewest executions, has the lowest." While it is true that there is a positive correlation between the existence of the death penalty and higher murder rates, this does not prove causation. It is more likely that the places that suffer from a high murder rate are therefore more likely to want the death penalty. Even abolitionists don't believe that ending the death penalty in the South would cause their murder rates to decrease.

Clever abolitionists who are aware of the deterrence effect will often make the nuanced distinction that "There is no *significant* deterrence effect." In the United States, we execute about 20-30 people a year. If each execution saved two innocent lives, that's only 40-60 people a year. Most people would probably agree that, technically, 40-60 fewer murders out of 16,000 annually is not "significant." But if two people close to you were murdered just so a convicted murderer didn't have to be executed, you would likely not be satisfied with the abolitionist's semantic game.

Some abolitionists will argue that, while the specific deterrence effect is undeniable, evidence for the general deterrence effect is "inconclusive." As mentioned at the beginning of this chapter, because we are unable to recreate death penalty scenarios, this is an intellectually honest position to maintain. However, it does acknowledge that some murders will be deterred (specific deterrence). It just states that we can't be certain how many *additional* murders will be avoided due to general deterrence. But if we are not certain, shouldn't we err on the side of protecting innocent human life from painful deaths than protect murderers from painless ones?

Abolishing the death penalty also leads to perverse incentives for criminals. Let's analyze a criminal who is engaging in the act of aggravated rape. Due to his criminal background and the extreme circumstances involved in the current crime, if he is caught he will receive life in prison. If there's no death penalty, then killing the rape victim will also just result in life in prison. Given that a dead rape victim can't testify in court, this provides a strong incentive for the rapist to kill his victim. Another example would be someone serving a life term in prison in a state without the death penalty. There is no significant deterrent for that person to not kill again in prison.[18]

The most troubling part about the abolitionist position on deterrence is illustrated with a hypothetical question: "Say it was 100 percent proven that for every convicted murderer executed, one innocent person was prevented from being murdered. Then would you favor the death penalty?" The vast majority of abolitionists I have asked, have answered, "No." This is indicative of the level of logic present in the leaders of their movement. Given the choice, they would prefer an innocent person be killed in a sudden and often painful way (and all the unrest that murder causes the victim's family and community), than have a convicted murderer be executed by lethal injection.[19] Even more frightening is that many leading abolitionists take this even further, preferring to have 100 innocent people murdered if it meant preventing just one murderer from being executed.

Again, the death penalty has an undeniable deterrent effect (specific deterrence). The only debate is whether it has an additional general

---

[18] Often times when these perverse incentives that would result from abolishing the death penalty are brought up, the abolitionist responds with something along the lines of, "Well, killing someone in prison doesn't really count. We're talking about innocent people in the streets being killed." This begs the question, "If it's not a big deal when someone in prison is killed, then what's the problem with the death penalty?"

[19] Not to be outdone, leading abolitionist Hugo Adam Bedau takes this absurd position to new lows. He states that he would oppose capital punishment even if it increased the homicide rate by 100% *or more!* With around 16,000 annual homicides in the U.S., that means he would prefer to have an additional 16,000 innocent people *or more* murdered every year, than have 20-30 convicted murderers executed annually.

Prominent abolitionists Charles Black, Ramsey Clark, and Henry Schwartzchild all say they would choose to have 100 innocent people murdered if it meant that one murderer was spared the death penalty.

deterrence effect. While all the available evidence points to the existence of a general deterrence effect, we cannot be absolutely certain given the limits of research methods.

Executing the Innocent

Here, it is important to distinguish between "innocent" and "wrongfully convicted." Our criminal justice system implements the most stringent burden of proof ever known to man: A unanimous verdict that the defendant is guilty beyond a reasonable doubt. Therefore, if just 1 out of 12 jurors think there is any level of reasonable doubt, the defendant is not convicted. This in no way means the defendant is likely innocent; that one juror could be 90% certain of his guilt. But, because there is some level of reasonable doubt to that one juror, the defendant is not convicted.

When you hear on the news that an "innocent" man was exonerated, it's almost always more accurate to say that he was "wrongfully convicted." Meaning, at his trial, none of the 12 jurors had any reasonable doubt regarding his guilt, but new evidence now casts some reasonable doubt. Again, this is very different from being innocent. Abolitionists who know better often intentionally blur this distinction to further their agenda. This deceptive strategy is effective because it only takes five words to say, "An innocent man was convicted." Conversely, as you can see from this chapter, it takes a lot more to explain why that is incorrect.[20]

The most popular research claiming innocence of those executed was a 1987 article by Bedau and Radelet, which alleged that 23 innocent people had been executed in the United States. However, the article provides only one example in the last 40 years, that of James Adams. Their allegation of Adams's innocence is based solely on his Petition for Execution Clemency, a document written by Adams's lawyers. When the facts of the case are looked at objectively, it becomes obvious that his innocence is unlikely. Adams was arrested possessing money stained with the murder victim's blood. He lied to the police, telling them that the blood was his. Adams's clothes were in his trunk with the victim's blood on them. The victim's eyeglasses were also in Adams's trunk. He told the

---

[20] Some organizations even name themselves after this misunderstanding. "The innocence project," for example, would more accurately be called, "The wrongfully convicted project."

police that the clothing and glasses were his but then, in court, said they were not. Multiple eyewitnesses saw Adams at the victim's house at the time of the murder. A few hours after the murder, Adams attempted to have his car painted a different color.

Aware that there is no conclusive evidence of an innocent man being executed in the last 40 years,[21] some abolitionists have continued to make the claim by attempting to change what the word innocent means. Prominent abolitionist Michael Radelet claimed that Ernest Dobbert was innocent of beating and choking his daughter to death (he also killed his son and tortured two other children), not because he didn't do it. Rather, because "maybe" Dobbert didn't deliberate long enough before killing his daughter. In this sense, Radelet claims, "Florida executed an innocent man."

---

[21] Note what I am not saying: I'm not saying that an innocent man was never executed in America in the 1800s. I'm not saying that it is per se impossible for an innocent man to be executed in 21st century America. I'm not even saying that an innocent man hasn't been executed in the last 40 years, just that there is no conclusive evidence of this happening. And finally, I'm not saying that in the last 40 years, no one was ever sentenced to death and then discovered to be innocent before being executed. In that final clarification, note that that scenario is not an argument against the death penalty. To the contrary, it shows that the stringent protections in place are working.

Life in Prison is worse than Death Penalty

Susan Milligan, an abolitionist writing for U.S. News and World Report, claims that life in prison is "much worse" than the death penalty.[22] Unlike many of the arguments presented here, this one is often not even honestly held by those who espouse it. If a life sentence is worse than the death penalty, then why would abolitionists argue against the death penalty?

Judy Clarke, the defense attorney in the Boston Marathon bomber trial, tried to argue this point in an attempt to spare her client the death penalty. Of course, if it were true that life in prison is worse than the death penalty, then it would be malpractice for her to pursue the more severe punishment. Clarke later contradicted herself when she pleaded for a life sentence because it "reflects justice and mercy." The jury was not persuaded by Clarke's reverse psychology and ultimately gave the Boston Marathon bomber the death penalty.

Some abolitionists are not willing to go to the extreme of saying that life in prison is worse than the death penalty, but do maintain that life in prison "might be a civilized equivalent to the death penalty—after all, people sentenced to life imprisonment have traditionally been regarded as 'civilly dead'."[23]

---

[22] This article also illustrates the disjointed logic for arguing that a life sentence is worse than the death penalty. The author is making a case for mercy on the murderer while at the same time arguing in favor of giving him a punishment "much worse" than death. As is standard in abolitionists' writings, this author also includes the recurrent fiction that there exists an option for life in prison, "with no hope of ever getting out."
Furthermore, this claim is even more nonsensical in light of all the abolitionists mentioned in footnote 19 who said they would prefer 100 innocent people be murdered if it saved a single murderer from being executed. If a life sentence is truly worse than execution, then these people would be willing to have 100 innocent people murdered in order to increase the punishment for someone on death row.

[23] Abolitionist Robert Johnson explains this in more detail: "[Prisoners] experience a permanent civil death, the death of freedom. The prison is their cemetery, a 6′ by 9′ cell their tomb. Interred in the name of justice, they are

Arbitrary Application

Abolitionists correctly point out that the death penalty is, in a way, arbitrarily applied in the U.S. For example, in 1998, after a routine traffic stop, Andrew Howard shot a police officer nine times. With the officer still alive, Howard reloaded and dealt a final, fatal blow after saying, "Die, fucker." The event was caught on the officer's dashboard camera. Because this tragic event happened in Georgia, Howard was executed. Had this event happened in Illinois (where there is no death penalty), the murderer could not have been executed. So in this limited sense, the application of the death penalty is arbitrary.

Having established the arbitrariness, the problem for the abolitionist is to show that just because the hypothetical cop killer in Illinois did not receive the punishment he deserved, that this somehow means the cop killer in Georgia also should not receive the punishment he deserves. When choosing between either one person not receiving their just punishment or nobody receiving their just punishment, it seems axiomatic that the former is preferable to the latter.

For an additional example, let's say Matt robs a bank on Monday and John robs a bank on Tuesday. The police officers make mistakes when gathering evidence against Matt, and he therefore is not tried for his crime. John is tried and convicted. Here, both Matt and John committed the exact same crime and Matt went free while John was punished. Therefore, this is arbitrary. However, would this scenario be improved by not giving John the punishment he deserves? Of course not!

---

consigned to mark the passage of their lives in the prison's peculiar dead time, which serves no larger human purpose and yields few rewards. In effect, they give their civil lives in return for the natural lives they have taken."

Excluding Abolitionist Jurors

During jury selection for a capital case, a potential juror who says they would refuse to apply the death penalty no matter what the situation is excluded from serving on the jury. This is a "for cause" dismissal and therefore can be used an unlimited number of times. Because women and African Americans are more likely than the general population to be against the death penalty, this results in an overall slightly disproportionate jury pool in capital cases. Questioning a potential juror about the death penalty is referred to as a "Witherspoon question" from the 1968 Supreme Court case of *Witherspoon v. Illinois*. A person who is opposed to the death penalty can still be allowed on a jury if, despite their personal convictions, they are willing to consider the death penalty as an option. Also, the flipside of "death-qualified juries" is rarely mentioned: That a potential juror who would *only* consider the death penalty and not a life sentence is also disqualified from the jury.

Abolitionists who disagree with the Witherspoon question point out that the "death qualified" juries it produces are too "conviction prone." But they never provide a suitable alternative (other than just doing away with the death penalty which is circular reasoning because that's the conclusion they are using this argument to arrive at). It would be a strange legal system indeed that allowed, say, jurors who admitted that they absolutely, under no circumstance, would impose a 10-year prison term, to serve on a trial where the prosecutor was seeking a 10-year prison term.

Other Countries

Abolitionists are quick to point out that countries like Iran, Somalia, and Nigeria have the death penalty and that America shouldn't be aligned with such barbaric cultures. They conveniently forget to mention that countries like Japan and Singapore also have the death penalty.

This line of reasoning is often presented in a misleading way, illustrated here by leading abolitionist Hugo Adam Bedau: "The rest of the civilized world openly and increasingly condemns our death penalty practices." This is simply not true. A majority of Canadians, Britains, Italians, and French want the death penalty reinstated. Joshua Marshall, a liberal columnist, explains the reality: "Europe doesn't have the death penalty because its political systems are less democratic, or at least more insulated from populists' impulses, than the U.S. government."[24]

I have yet to meet an abolitionist who would consider changing his position if the international makeup of death penalty countries significantly changed. That's because, despite bringing it up, the abolitionist recognizes that the issue of whether America should have the death penalty stands on its own merits, regardless of what other countries decide to do.

---

[24] Germany even banned Turkish consulates and embassies to act as polling stations for purposes of reinstating the death penalty in Turkey. A government spokesman said that it was "politically inconceivable" that they would allow Turkish citizens in Germany to vote for the death penalty. He continued, "We will use all legal means to prevent something like this. Austria said they would also ban Turks from voting on the issue."

Saving Money

The premise to this argument is accurate: It is cheaper, on average, to sentence someone to life without parole than to execute them.[25] However, the conclusion that we therefore shouldn't execute people doesn't follow. The reason it is so expensive is because of all the legal protections involved. This goes against the abolitionist's claim that those who commit capital offenses don't receive adequate legal representation. Furthermore, cost differences among different punishments are certainly not unique to capital offenses; you can always save money by giving a criminal less than they deserve. Would you want to be the one to tell the victim's family that, while they didn't receive justice, we probably saved the government some money?

Like most of the abolitionist arguments in this book, if this was negated and the death penalty was somehow cheaper than life sentences, it would have no effect on their desire to end the death penalty.

---

[25] However, this does not factor in the additional costs, financial and otherwise, involved with murderers serving life sentences who kill again.

Life Sentence as Suitable Alternative

In 1974, Willie Horton robbed a convenience store. After the 17-year-old clerk fully complied, Horton nevertheless fatally stabbed him 19 times. He then discarded the body by folding it in half and stuffing it in a trash can. He was convicted and sentenced to "life imprisonment without the possibility of parole." Later, Horton was intentionally given an unsupervised weekend off from prison. He used this opportunity to break into the house of a young couple, stabbing the man and repeatedly raping the woman.[26] The case of Willie Horton is one of many grim reminders that nothing short of the death penalty can guaranty that a murderer will not strike again.

The story of Kenneth Allen McDuff, and the countless lives he affected, is another cautionary tale about what can happen when someone is not given the death penalty. McDuff raped, tortured, and murdered at least nine women in the 90s. He later said that "Killing a woman is like killing a chicken... they both squawk." The most tragic aspect to this story is that it could have easily been avoided. In the 60s, McDuff was sentenced to death for killing two teenage boys and brutally raping a teenage girl before killing her by crushing her neck. McDuff had his sentence commuted when the Supreme Court banned all executions in 1972. He was then released in 1989, where he quickly went back to his modus operandi.

Despite the reality of lifers killing again, abolitionists attempt to present a choice between the death penalty and locking someone up and never

---

[26] The Willie Horton fiasco was made famous because future Democratic presidential candidate Michael Dukakis was largely to blame. The Massachusetts legislature passed a bill excluding first-degree murderers from the furlough program. Then Governor Dukakis vetoed the bill, thus allowing Horton, who was serving a life sentence without the possibility of parole, to have unsupervised weekends off from prison. To this day, Horton portrays himself as the biggest victim in the matter because an anti-Dukakis advertisement displayed an unedited photograph of him (he is African American), and referred to him as "Willie" instead of "William." He also laments that his civil rights are being violated because he is not allowed to get a college degree while in prison.

letting them out. As this chapter illustrates, this is a fiction. Furthermore, although they are reluctant to admit it, many abolitionists also want to do away with life sentences. Former ACLU president Nadine Strossen was upfront about her opinion that life sentences violate the 8th Amendment's Cruel and Unusual Clause and therefore should be banned. Countries like Norway have a 21 year maximum prison sentence, which is what Anders Brevik received after killing 77 people there in 2012.

Conclusion

By presenting an often underrepresented side, I hope this book has provided you a more well-rounded view on this controversial topic. [27]

If you have come across an abolitionist argument that is not included in this book, or want to provide constructive feedback of any kind, please leave a review on Amazon and I will be happy to respond.

---

[27] On a somewhat related note, you can see the transcript for all the last words of those executed in Texas at https://www.tdcj.state.tx.us/death_row/dr_executed_offenders.html. Also included is information about the person they murdered. While this has no bearing on whether capital punishment should be allowed, it's a powerful glimpse into the death penalty process.

Printed in Great Britain
by Amazon

18184082R00031